Consciously

CONSCIOUSLY 21

SAUN-JAYE BROWN

First published in 2017

Copyright ©Tamarind Hill Press 2017

The moral right of Saun-Jaye Brown to be identified as the author of this work has been asserted in accordance with the Copyright, Design and Patents Act of 1988.

All rights reserved. No part of this publication may be reproduced, stored in a retrievable system, or transmitted in any form or by any means, electronic, mechanical, photocopying, recording or otherwise, without the prior permission of the author and copyright owner.

ISBN
978-1-9998152-0-2

TAMRiND HiLL
.PRESS

Acknowledgement

The starting point for this book came alive during a discussion with my sister Kemone; to her I will always be grateful.

I would like to express my gratitude to the many people who were instrumental in making this happen; to all those who provided support, and offered advice and comments.

I owe a huge thank you to my editors and sisters Tashana and Kemone for their constant belief in me.

Thank you, Rochelle Dawkins, my great friend, for your generous readings and encouragement.

Special thanks to my mother, brother, sisters and father for providing inspiration and support; you all made this possible. To my friends, thank you for your love, advice and friendship.

Finally, thank you God, for providing me with this opportunity.

CONSCIOUSLY 21

SAUN-JAYE BROWN

"21
The time in which we worry about the future
Where we pay keen attention to the years that are
up next
Time for adulting
But being an adult is never timeless"

Mirror Mirror

They say self-love is the best kind of love.

Mirror mirror on the wall
It once scared me to look at you at all
The image I used to see
Is no longer distorted to me
For my mind is now shackle free.
You showed me all my flaws
Ushered me to love them all
You showed me how my smile illuminates a room
Like a rich lily that forever blooms
You have comforted me in such a way
That I have grown to love the skin I am in
Through you, my glow surely can begin.

Mirror mirror
As I stare at my reflection
I will no longer starve for perfection
I will no longer be bounded by such pain
I will no longer feel the weight of those chains.
Staring at me
Looking into you so deep
Has somehow brought me peace
Self-love is all I need.

Mirror mirror
You tell me that I am beautiful
And I once thought that was refutable

But as I look deeper
Every glowing line gets clearer
Making me love me even harder
You remind me that:
My arms are not too fat
My legs are not too long
My hips are not too wide
My chest is not too flat
You remind me that:
I mustn't crave for the body of someone else
I must crave only the body of myself.

"Forgotten are the devoting fathers"

I Bear Your Imprint
From her lips to my notebook

Dear Elijah Malachi Parkes
You beautiful child of mine
I wish I could have seen you
Stretch those little arms and smile
Gone is my little baby boy
Chosen by God to fly
Like those beautiful clouds shining
Right before my eyes
HE has taken you to the skies.

My dearest Elijah
You will forever live
Inside me and our family too
For we bear the imprint of you
Your name
It sings to our souls
Never failing to bring music to our ears
Harvesting the love that each letter bears.

I never got the chance to hold you
Or to see those little toes
I never got the chance to kiss that handsome face of yours
Or to watch you sleep for what would seem like hours
I never got the chance to look into your eyes
Or to hear your cries

I never got the chance to kiss you on your cute little button nose
I won't get to watch you grow

My dearest Elijah
That once grew inside me
All I have of you are memories
Ones that I will forever cherish
Memories of a beating heart
And a love that knew no boundaries from the start
Memories of someone who brought me immense joy
My beautiful baby boy
Memories that I will water and feed with love
For they must blossom
Just like you would have blossomed, my dove
I'll forever tend these memories
And they will bloom
Bearing the imprint of you.

For my dear sister Tashana
With Love♥

Mama

21 Reasons why:

1. It was her who heroically bore me for 9 months
2. It was only her who delivered me into this world all the while bearing the most agonizing pain that only she and others like her can describe
3. It was her who was created to void me of hunger with the nourishments from her breasts
4. It was her who taught me how to crawl and take my first steps into this world
5. It was her who foraged the earth to feed me

6. It was her who enslaved herself in work to earn every penny needed for the primary principle of living called survival
7. It was her who without end stood by my side day and night protecting me from even the most unthreatening of things
8. It was her who prayed to God for my betterment
9. It was her who believed in my voice
10. It was her who fought endlessly to ensure that my dreams however silly weren't cast aside
11. It was her who was there to congratulate me in all that I have accomplished

12. It was her who so selflessly showered me with countless blessings in all my endeavours

13. It was her who so immortally loved me as her child

14. It was her who dedicated every beat of her heart to my being

15. It was her who fulfilled her duty to guide me with every sweat and every tear

16. It was her who so timelessly nourished my mind, body and soul

17. It is her who is the beacon that glows in the darkness should I ever be led astray

18. It is her who has taught me to take giant strides in life

19. It is her who pushes me to fly despite gravity's mission to hold me down

20. It is only her who understands my tears when I become weary

21. It is her who has shown me what a mother's love is.

The underdogs

The word father has become such a forgotten word
Only to receive the spotlight 2 out of 365 days of the year
Happy Birthday Father!
Happy Father's day!
Why such little focus on the good men do

Some do not remember it
Others neglect it
Others are not especially committed to it

Fathers help to create something beautiful
Embodying creation and life
They are what no one writes about:
    They are the little pebbles lost in the sand
    They are the unsung lyrics of that forgotten song
    They are the worn clothes that we toss
    They are the unthought and the unspoken of

Forgotten are the devoting fathers
Who spend their time selflessly working
Their own dreams rarely spoken
Never looking for praises
As they live for us and break no promises
Their wants are very few
Only to receive rare moments
Of thank you

For the unparalleled commitment
Why must the good ones face such punishment?
Forgotten is sacrificed time
Their outstanding performance of hard work
Shown in bloodshot eyes
But only for them to be cast aside

A Father's Apology to his Daughter

"It's a girl" the nurse announced
A beautiful healthy baby girl
With a cry as loud as a thunderstorm
Yet you were so small
delicate and warm

I never knew men could have butterflies
But on those days
When I looked into your hazel eyes
I felt in the pit of my stomach
Their constant flutter

"You'll be a great dad!" everyone said
So sure of their prediction
Yet here I am
Apologizing for failing miserably
Hurting you terribly

I hear the constant echo
"Don't worry cupcake daddy will always be here"
But today as you turn 18
All grown up
A stranger you are to me

The smudges on this paper you see
Are the results of my pitiful crying, weeping
Drowning in sorrows
How can I even begin to say sorry?
How can I even expect you to forgive me?

I still listen for your melodious laughter
But all I hear is silence
Like that wistful night when I left
One I will always regret
Fear knocked on the door and I fled

Your first day of preschool
I would have dropped you off
Kissed and told you I loved you
You'd cry
But the days would pass
And soon all I'd get
Is a wave goodbye

"Daddy Daddy!" you would say
Oh how I long for that day
But I know you may never shout that name
"Cupcake," would be the response
"come tell Daddy all about your day"

I am trying to fight back the tears
But my eyes sting
And down they come in floods

Please forgive me
I am nothing but sorry
It hurts that I can't touch you
It hurts that I can't see you

Sorry, I say over and over again
And I accept that you may not want to hear it

But my sincerest apologies
My dearest daughter

I am nothing,
But a man with regrets
A heartbroken "father"
Who's sorry for not being there
I'm the coward who left

*"My blackness does not emanate
Through soft natural curls"*

Bleeding Melanin

The rich melanin in our skin
Let's embrace it
Our honey brown and cocoa shade don't you see
it's perfect
The pigment of our skin
Should have never been an issue
The tint of our skin
Look at how it shines and glistens
In the light, our skin is a magical sight to see
For we are a special kind of breed
Our melanin how it does glow
A beauty that no painter could ever show
Is that why we are rarely featured in your
magazines?

Melanin kings and queens
We are spoonsful of dripping honey
We are black without apology
Our dark skins are like charcoal
A glorious consistency
Symbolizing the strength of our people
And of course, their tenacity
We were beautifully woven
Chocolate, caramel and brown sugar
Symbolizing every hardship that our black family
had to suffer
This skin that we wear
Represents every sweat, blood and tear
Our skin is history

The melanin, it tells a story
Light skinned-dark skinned
Mahogany, ebony
It matters not, the shade
We are **black**
And to this I will never take offence
For we represent strength, grace and excellence.

Dear Black Girl

Dear Black Girl,
    You have fallen victim
    To the media's restrictions and expectations
    You have fallen victim
    To society's perpetuation
    Of reality
    Where they tell you to believe
    In something that is nothing more than a fallacy

Dear Black Girl,
    It is time to realize
    With your own eyes
    The beauty of
    Your dark skin
    Infused with rich melanin
    The chocolate overflowing in your veins
    Your confident walk so strong it stains
    With your black hair
    Glowing, so thick, coarse and nappy
    Your pearly whites
    Shining when you're ever so happy
    Your eloquent speech
    Spilling from your full plump lips
    Your enthralling brown eyes
    Baring your beauty

Dear Black Girl,
    You are royalty
    Don't let anyone tell you
    "Oh for a black girl you are so pretty"
    You are beautiful and
    It is as simple as that
    Your cornrows are not ghetto
    They are high fashion
    And not only when worn by the 'white' person
    Your ass is not too round
    Drown out their lies
    For they visit surgeons to add a few pounds

Dear Black Girl,
    You are not a stereotype
    You are gorgeous
    And so is your mind
    You possess intelligence
    Within you there is magnificence
    Don't let being black in a world full of light
    Force you into a corner where you cannot fight
    Approval is not something you need,
    They may criticize or even compliment as they please,
    But wear you like no other model on a runway ever could
    For you are beautiful
    From your lips, to your hair, to your skin

From the light, to the golden and the cocoa
brown
They cannot touch you
The sun it loves you.

Sincerely,
Another black girl

Natural or Perm (Am I Less Black)

As a black woman
In today's society
I've come to expect the question
When are you going to do the big chop?
When are you going to bring those curls back?
I'm a black woman
With straightened hair
Better yet I'm a black woman
With white people's hair
That's what you call it isn't it?
My blackness does not emanate
Through soft natural curls
Why have you declared war on my perm?
Am I less black?

Because of how I choose
To deal with my God-given roots
Is it 'blacker' to embrace the kink?
Am I committing a felony?
Because I have a hair preference which is not coily
Am I committing a crime against my own ethnicity?
Should I be convicted by the "natural hair grand jury"?
Don't get me wrong
I give props to those embracing their sea of curls
But am I less black?
Because I chemically change mine

Other races do it
Yet nobody puts up a fuss
Should I be stripped of my ability to self-express?
Should I be stripped of my black identity?
Because I don't follow your projections
Of how I should be black
You embrace the natural goodness
While I relax
You wear those coils
Like a badge of honour
But hair isn't the symbol of black power
Tell me what's so wrong with having a relaxer

So I sport a perm
Am I less black?
So I don't twist out, detangle and roll?
Am I less black
So I take a hot comb to those coils
Am I less black?
When it comes to 'black' hair
A point of view other than natural is like betrayal
For **natural** is the new *black*

*"You have been taught to hate them
To perpetuate exclusion and the divide"*

A Mission for True Freedom

There is a critical question to be asked
Is true freedom
Not caring what others think of you?
Or
Is true freedom
Fighting for what you believe in without question or pause?

On our path to freedom we must consider:
We will never know true freedom until
We learn to love ourselves
We will never know true freedom until
We stop spending most of our lives searching for something else
We will never know true freedom until
We escape the need for others to love us
We will never know true freedom until
We are liberated from others expectations of us
We will never know true freedom until
We dream and achieve the impossible dream
We will never know true freedom until
We realize that no risk taken is too extreme
We will never know true freedom until
We defeat that unbeatable foe
We will never know true freedom until
We learn to simply just let go
We will never know true freedom until
We learn to control how we react to the world around us

We will never know true freedom until
We stop holding on to the past and letting it define
us
We will never know true freedom until
We stop worrying about the outcome of tomorrow
We will never know true freedom until
We let go of that never-ending cloud of sorrow
We will never know true freedom until
We let go of what we cannot change

The truth is we can never be truly free
By just not being slaves
We are truly free when we are also no longer
masters
We are truly free when we appreciate that
Everyone deserves to be free according to their
own understanding

Letter to the Homophobe

Dear Sir/Madam,
   They are humans.

   It is because of people like you
   Why *hundreds* are scorned
   It is because of people like you
   Why a family now has to mourn
   It is because of people like you
   Why *he* thought suicide was *his* only option
   It is because of people like you
   Why *she's* on the road to destruction
   It is because of people like you
   Why *they* cower in fear
   It is because of people like you
   Why insults, cuts, and bruises are what *they* have to bear.

   You insult *him* because of *his* sexuality?
   Are you that afraid, that *he* might threaten your masculinity?
   You hurl at *him*, the word fag, as though it were stone
   Why must *he* suffer for whatever insecurities you have of your own?
   You tell *her she's* broken
   Who are you to judge *her* because *she* decided to be true and open?
   You make it clear that *her* happiness upsets you

How can this be fair in your view?
You make it your duty to bring *her* down
Does it make you feel powerful to be the cause of *her* frown?

Humanity encompasses **every man** and **every woman**
Yet you view "*them*" as brutes, irrelevant
You force *him* to be smaller
Caging *him* with the words you holler
You force *her* to feel voiceless
She must be voiceless, so *her* punishment is less
Your eyes pierce *them*, like a disease
An affliction, ready to bring you down to your knees
Your words are like daggers, every day they only get sharper
Leaving *them* with scars that can't be wiped out, like a permanent marker
Scars engraved like tattoos
All in the name of your biased views

Before you write back
With a rhetoric attack
Pause
Stop for a minute
It might also be a good idea to take a few deep breaths

With a clear mind and heart, you would actually see
They are no different from you or me
Like *them* you're a victim
The difference is you continue to choose to be
You have been taught to hate *them*
To perpetuate exclusion and the divide

Now, I will leave you with this
How would you want the world to react
If something as natural
As the fact that you breathe
Was soon stigmatized
Even illegalized

With regards,
Watching Eyes of the Conscious Mind

A Poor Man's Prayer

Dear Lord, I come to you my body weak and starving
My throat parched and burning
My fellow brothers and sisters they hear my pleas
But pass me by on my bended knees
Here I am curled upon on this street
With my tattered clothes, and bare, cold feet
Help me oh Lord
For my skin is peeling
And my hands and feet burn
As I face agony at every turn
Lord I ask you to hear me
For the rest they ignore my cries
Spare change lady?
But returned is disgust shown in her eyes
Father I am alone
Each day I wander to and fro
Consumed by hunger
I am forced to ponder
When my time will come
As the days close in
I am drenched with darkness and dread
As I lay on this pavement that I must call my bed
Lord I come to you, weak and thirsty.

Equality (We are one)

Black, White, Mongoloid
Man or Woman
African, Asian, Hispanic, European
We are beautifully different
Led to believe in the conspiracy that difference is ugly
One always better than the other

Man or woman
Boy or Girl
How are we not the same?
We are all people
Yet not valued the same
We are all puppets
Bounded by the hands of society
As it pushes and pulls us in whatever direction it chooses

Why must we be divided?
 By race, religion or sexuality
Allowing society to put its stamp on us
Teaching us to injure, hurt and insult those who are different

Humans
We all are
This is what we must be constantly taught
Stop filling us with anger and hate
Always finding ways to discriminate

Stop with the prejudices and judgments
Why do we continue to cut, divide and separate?

We are equal whether we accept it or not
Death knows no boundaries
It cares not of our differences
It takes us one by one
Regardless of colour, race, religion, or sexual orientation
Man or woman, young or old
Death is equal

*"I choose to wear my clothes based on my own needs and preferences
And not when I think men demand it"*

Confessions of the Scarred

Do you know the definition of
Pain?
Do you know the definition of
Hurt?
Pain: the never thinning ache that my heart
endures
Hurt: the constant bruising of my flesh and my
mind.

We are told to wait until marriage
Yet we are sexualized beings
We are told to be submissive to the opposite sex
Our mind first, then our body next
We are drugged and taken advantage of
And they blame our clothes or lack thereof
It doesn't matter that we say no
For I am woman
And
My lips must be sucked
My breast must be touched
AND
My *cherry* must be plucked.

Your fingertips,
They trace down my back
Pulling me closer and closer
As you shove apart my knees
You ignore all my pleas
"Please don't sir"

But you ignore every cringe and every shudder
You fit yourself between my legs
Shoving your tongue down my throat
I gasp for air
But you continue on
Whatever mercy you should have shown me long gone

Our tongues are cut out
So our voices cannot be heard
We are silenced
We mustn't utter a word
Our throats bear the marks of your hands
When we don't fulfil your demands
And as if mocking my frail hopes
Your hands they wrap tighter like ropes
Their sheer purpose to suffocate
Each breath slowly fading away

Am I not a person to you?
Think of your mother
Your sister
What about your own daughter?
Why do you bash me so?
Like it is an innate need
Why must you misuse me?
Like my body and soul are yours on which to feed

Do you forget that your daughter, your mother, your sister
Live in the same skin as me?

How dare you grab a woman?
Forcing her to witness
The damage of your uninvited hands?
Your abusing cage
Rendering us afraid
We are violated and used
Why must we face this abuse?
Our protectors you should be
Yet you choose not to protect but instead to scar me
We are not your public property
We never will be.

Dress Code

Dresser drawers open
Beds assaulted by flying clothes
Shoes litter the floors
Nothing fits
Nothing is perfect enough
Nothing I put on is quite right
Everything so bland
I'm not seeking to be desired

Now it dawns on me
The issue is not the clothes, bags or shoes I'm seeing
But how do I dress
So that it doesn't seem I'm seeking to bring every man to concupiscence

Too many articles
Telling us to dress to impress men
Too many individuals
Believing all the nonsense

I dress for me
Not anyone else

Why do you constantly think
My sleek sexy jeans caressing my thighs
Is being worn to please his predatory eyes?
Eyes that rake me over as men undress me in their minds

My mini skirt
Is not for men's crudely insulting stares
Nor is it a medium for them to sexualize the legs
they bare
It helps me feel empowered in my own body
It is something that helps me celebrate my
sexuality

My low-cut shirt
Is an expression of fashion and my sassiness
It's not for you to ogle my breasts
With your insufferable brashness

My bodycon dress
Embracing my every curve
Is not to be used as a mechanism for you to define
me or my body

My fierce red heels
Are not meant to please men or enhance my sex
appeal for him to be pleased
They are symbols of my strength and boldness
They are not to "attract the male eye"
Nor are they to satisfy
His erotic fantasies

I did not squeeze into this tiny size 2 dress
So, you can stare at my ass
And use not your hands but your eyes to violate me
with your uninvited caress

I choose to wear my clothes based on my own
needs and preferences
And not when I think men demand it
I dress to express myself for me
Simply for comfort, freedom and individuality

Ethos of the Woman

The ethos of a woman is her true beauty,
So beautiful; a blind man can see
As she lights up a room
With her captivating face
And a contagious smile that takes you to the highest place.

The ethos of a woman is her profound ability to withstand pain
As much or more others would complain
It's how underneath all the blood loss and screams a woman is turned into a mother
It's her motherly love that will make you know you need no other.
It's the humble heart she shows
Breathing life into others, warming souls when their spirits feel low

The ethos of a woman is restraining her tongue for no one
It's her will to ignore cat calls and insults flung
It's the life that is conveyed in her star dust eyes
A vibrancy that will light up even the darkest of skies

The ethos of a woman is the inspirational words she bestows upon her lover
Drawing him in with her powerful aura
It's her soothing touch

That stirs up emotions making him want her so much
It's the alluring curves of her body that makes him drool,
It's her gorgeous legs that make him beg

The ethos of a woman is her intellectual mind
Emitting brilliance with every word she speaks
It's the passion in her beliefs
It's how she is driven by assurance
It's how she doesn't wish to be someone else,
The ethos of the woman is not limited to the vocabulary of motherly, soft, and gentleness
The ethos of the woman is the greatness that she bleeds.

Innocence Lost

Innocence is the definition of childhood
Children, untainted by the world's darkest secrets
Such a marvellous thing
To be pure and free of darkness
To see only beauty
Laid out before your eyes
But that gift of innocence is taken, lost
By experiences that always come at a cost

You draw them in
With compliments and lies
You capture them
With gifts, money and affection
Preying on their innocence
As you pretend to care
Charming them
They smile with hope
As you lead them away
From whatever troubles they have

Their little throats
Not prepared for the smoke or tequila
Every burn reminding them of what is to come next
Lips sporting different colours
Fiery red, sea blue and glowing purple
Skirts short as patience
Shirts with the top button undone
Well-tailored pants hiding every bruise
Feet sporting the most sought-after shoes

The hair on their heads perfectly groomed
As you pass them around
Room to room
Unbuttoning their souls

You provide them with glitter and gold
You lay down your money
Fling out your cash
And in exchange they strip for you
All the while stripping their innocence
Their childlike traits extracted from their very soul
Unaware that they are prisoners to you and their own bodies
Forcibly manipulated by another

Their bodies flaunted
Shredding every ounce of innocence
They are vessels for your own dark desires
Captives and hostages of
Your endless and vicious games
Their once fiery souls missing
As they become imprisoned
By your agonizing playtime
Innocence lost, all for someone who they called friend's pleasure.

Betrayed

You came to me
Bearing nothing but love and compassion
My mind, it raced ahead and excitingly said,
"All of our life
Where has this man been?
Please! Oh please let him in"
And so my heart opened its gates
Not knowing the pain to come, that hurt awaits

You brought me flowers,
Bouquets hosting every kind
And I thought to myself
This man must truly be mine
He must love me, he must care
Never thinking for a second
That,
I wasn't the only one you called "dear"

You showered me with gifts
The most expensive of things
My heart it would gladly sing,
"He's the perfect man,
The one who will soon ask for your hand"
But I have now come to realize
Those gifts of yours were all wrapped in lies

You stopped coming home
And I would sit there
ALONE

Waiting and hoping
But mostly hoping
Please don't let him be with her
My lonely heart it wondered
Is she what you prefer?

Nights upon nights
I waited for you
For months I bore,
The pain, the hurt, the deceit,
For years I stayed feeling incomplete
A hollow shell
Feeling like this is hell, MY hell

I now know that I deserve better
More than what you gave me
For what you gave me
Was never love
You were nothing but a diseased infection
With all your lies, deceit and deception
I may have suffered at your hands
But I have to thank you though
Because I learned that
I am a beautiful flower that must grow
Just like "the mighty oaks from little acorns grow"

You betrayed me
But I know now
Betrayal is nothing
It may hit blow by blow
But it has no power

For when I look at myself
What I used to see in the mirror
I see no more
Not the girl who's heart was stomped on
For that girl is long gone
Awaken
Is a strong woman

My Friend Jane

It's time she said,
Time for what?
Time to roll up, light up and smoke up.

I was only 16,
When she welcomed me to a sight unseen,
Selling lies that had me mesmerized,
Engulfed by her beauty, I was hypnotized.

School became a thing of the past,
For with my friend Jane I was having a blast,
She took me to places you wouldn't believe,
I was young, tender hearted and so naïve.

At times she would blow me up,
Other times she calmed my nerves with just one puff,
She was the queen of seduction,
Such poise and perfection.

What she didn't tell me,
Was how dangerous she could be,
For that Jane you see,
Started playing naughty tricks on me.

My lungs and her smoke in a deep romance,
Pulling me in as she does that intimate, intense and intriguing dance,

Tricky little thing she was, for my heart rate began to increase,
My blood pressure and blood sugar, they knew no peace.

With Jane I started eating more,
And sleeping less,
The kisses from her smoke, they stole my breath,
Little did I know those kisses I would soon regret.

I'm James, and you are?
Paranoia, but don't worry I'm a friend of Jane's,
I'm here to rid you of your friends,
And play games with your brain.

Knock knock?
Who's there?
Nobody.
Nobody who?
Nobody it's just you.

After continuous using,
And abusing,
I found myself at the end of the road with an addiction,
To her alone I gave my full submission.

Real and unreal,
I can't tell the difference,
My mind it needs to be silenced.
I've lost myself,

I really do seem like someone else,
My friend Jane,
Providing me with pleasure, spiked with pain.

*"And knowing this, she travels the path of victory
Never once doubting her capability"*

For You My Sister

As I sit here writing
I wonder what I should say
To a sister who brings me joy
That will forever stay
I can't seem to find the right words
For no words will do you justice
It's funny because there's so much to tell you
And a million things come to mind when I think of you
But what I should say, I have no clue.
I will try my best though
For the love I have for you, you have to know
So here I go

I've known you for 21 years
And in that time, we've shared hugs, kisses, laughter and tears.
My dearest sister
The angel in disguise
There is very little point to think otherwise
I know you are so far away
But in my heart you will forever stay
In there you have the biggest room
Until the day I meet my tomb
Maybe even then
I'd still keep you close.

My darling sister
So one of a kind

Like that beautiful melody
That's so hard to find
You are a most precious treasure
And they can search well, but to you no one will measure
You've fought so many battles
For some you weren't ready
But leave it to you my sister
To hit back hard and steady
You fight hard, like the champion you are
Showing time and time again
That you can bear it all

You fill my heart with love
And there's nothing I could want more
You fill my life with laughs and joy
A golden bond that none can destroy
You fill me with life
Because of you I know no strife
You fill my world with light
Like the beautiful stars, immovable and bright
There's not much left to say
Except that
I love you
I pray you find peace, love and happiness
Like you deserve
Until then, I will be the one to make you smile
Because I would go the extra mile
For you my sister.

High on Ambition

She's hooked
Just one shot
And she's in
Too powerful a feeling
To pass up
Its warmth melts away her doubts
It beckons to her
Drawing her in
As it lingers in the air
A gentle touch
And she feels its electricity coursing through her veins
Electricity holding a promise of success
She takes it all in, in silent acquiescence
She is ravenous
Yearning to satiate her hunger
She is consumed.

Consumed by determination
As she chases a career
Instead of chasing a man
She knows she can do so much
Before a guy puts a ring on her finger
She knows her 20s is the perfect time for her to chase her dreams
Her eyes are set on that broad pathway
As she knows failure to be the place where goals are non-existent
She sees a successful future in the distance

And knowing this, she travels the path of victory
Never once doubting her capability
I applaud her
High on ambition
As she looks to no guy to encourage her
She refuses to live in the comfort of a man
Because she knows that it does not require one
To realize her skills, talents and potential
She does not look for a man to make her bank account high
For she is nothing but confident and independent
I applaud the girl
Who sees success as the mission
Her first priority education
Her inspiration
Ambition.

Consciously 21

21
The turning point of youth
Where we experience the conflict of being young
Repressed by the idea
That the most difficult part of being young is
Figuring out what to do as we get older
Oppressed by age and time
Time our greatest enemy
Time the undefeated adversary

We couldn't wait to get older
We couldn't wait to be mature
Craving the supposed freedom that comes with
Being 21
We no longer dance on the edge of
Adolescence and adulthood
From here, every year is a step closer
To starting a real career
Travelling a real path in life
Plagued with decisions
Not about which bar to turn up to on Friday night

But where to go to grad school
Where to live after graduation
Face to face with the reality of life
The present once significant
Is now of less concern in comparison to the rest
As we struggle to figure out the future
And long for the past

Are we up to everyone else's expectations?
Does our maturity level match that which it should be?
We no longer play outside or run around
The world is not so simple anymore
Games we used play
Tag, hide and seek and catch
Now replaced with
Games of "What do you want to do with your life?"
Having responsibilities,
Working to save money
At this point we realize our time is not unlimited
We don't stay the same

21
The time in which we worry about the future
Where we pay keen attention to the years that are up next
Time for **adulting**
But being an adult is never timeless
Time to confront the idea that our clock might just run out.

"for my mind is now shackle free"

TAMRiND HiLL
.PRESS

www.ingramcontent.com/pod-product-compliance
Lightning Source LLC
Chambersburg PA
CBHW050044080526
44586CB00014B/1455